Luther

Luther

Thomas M. Lindsay

WIPF & STOCK · Eugene, Oregon

Wipf and Stock Publishers
199 W 8th Ave, Suite 3
Eugene, OR 97401

Luther
By Lindsay, Thomas M.
ISBN 13: 978-1-5326-1604-4
Publication date 2/1/2017
Previously published by Cambridge University Press, 1934

LUTHER.

THE Reformation of the sixteenth century had its birth and growth in a union of spiritual and secular forces such as the world has seldom seen at any other period of its history. On the secular side, the times were full of new movements, intellectual and moral, political, social, and economic; and spiritual forces were everywhere at work, which aimed at making religion the birthright and possession of the common man— whether king, noble, burgher, artisan, or peasant—as well as of the ecclesiastic, a possession which should directly promote a worthy life within the family and the State. These religious impulses had all a peculiar democratic element and were able to impregnate with passion and, for a time, to fuse together the secular forces of the period. Hence their importance historically. If the main defect in the earlier histories of the Reformation has been to neglect the secular sides of the movement, it is possible that more recent historians have been too apt to ignore the religious element which was a real power.

It may be an exaggeration to say, as is sometimes done, that this religious side of the Reformation began in the inward religious growth of a single personality—the river comes from a thousand nameless rills and not only from one selected fountain-head; yet Luther was so prominent a figure that the impulses in his religious life may be taken as the type of forces which were at work over a wide area, and the history of these forces may be fitly described in tracing the genesis and growth of his religious opinions from his early years to his struggle against Indulgences.

The real roots of the religious life of Luther must be sought for in the family and in the popular religious life of the times. What had Luther and Myconius and hundreds of other boys of the peasant and burgher classes been taught by their parents within the family, and what religious influences met them in high-school and University? Fortunately the writings of the leaders of the new religious movement abound in biographical details; and the recent labours of German historians enable us to form some idea of the discordant elements in the religious life at the close of the fifteenth century.

The religion taught by parents to children in pious German families seems to have been simple, unaffected and evangelical. Myconius relates how his father, a burgher, was accustomed to expound the Apostles' Creed to the boy and to tell him that Jesus Christ was the Saviour from all sins; that the one thing needed to obtain God's pardon for sins was to pray and to trust; and how he insisted above all that the forgiveness of God was a free gift, bestowed without fee by God on man for the sake of what Christ had done. Little books suitable for family instruction were in circulation in which were printed the Creed, the Lord's Prayer, the Ten Commandments, and sometimes one or two Psalms in the German tongue. Simple catechisms and other small books of devotion seem to have been in circulation which were full of very simple evangelical teaching. It is probable that Luther repeated a great deal of what was commonly taught to children in his own earliest years, when, in later days, he himself wrote little books for the young. Traces of this simple family piety, which insisted that all holiness came from "trusting in the holy passion of Christ," and that nothing which the sinner could do for himself availed anything, may be found all down the stream of medieval religious life in the most popular hymns and in the sermons of the great revival preachers.

The latter half of the fifteenth century saw the growth of a form of piety very different from that simple household religion. A strange terror seemed to brood over the people. The plague came periodically into the crowded and badly drained towns; new diseases made their appearance and added to the prevailing fear; the dread of a Turkish invasion seemed to be prevalent—mothers scared their children by naming the Turks, and in hundreds of German parishes the bells tolled in the village steeples calling the people to pray to God to deliver them from Turkish raids. This prevailing fear bred a strange restlessness. Crowds of pilgrims thronged the highways, trudging from shrine to shrine, hoping to get deliverance from fear and assurance of pardon for sins. Princes who could afford a sufficiently large armed guard visited the holy places in Palestine and brought back relics which they stored in their private chapels; the lesser nobility and the richer burghers made pilgrimages to Rome, especially during the Jubilee years, which became somewhat frequent in the later Middle Ages, and secured indulgences by visiting and praying before the several shrines in the Holy City. For the common folk of Germany, in the last decades of the fifteenth century, the favourite place of pilgrimage was Compostella in Spain, and, in the second degree, Einsiedeln in Switzerland. It was said that the bones of St James the Brother of our Lord had been brought from Palestine to Compostella; and the shrine numbered its pilgrims by the hundred thousand a year. So famous and frequented was this place of pilgrimage that a special, one might almost say a professional, class of pilgrims came into existence, the *Jacobsbrüder*, who were continually on the roads coming to or from Compostella, seeking to win pardon for themselves or others by their wandering devotion.

Sometimes the desire to go on pilgrimage became almost an epidemic. Bands of children thronged the roads, bareheaded and clad in nothing but their shirts; women left their families and men deserted their work. In vain preachers of morals like Geiler von Kaisersberg denounced the practice and said that on pilgrimages more sinners were created than sins pardoned. The terror swayed men and they fled to shrines where they believed they could find forgiveness; the pilgrimage songs make a small literature; and pilgrim guide-books, like the *Mirabilia Romae* and *Die Walfart und Strasse zu Sant Jacob*, appeared in many languages.

This revival of religion had its special effect on men destined to a religious life. The secular clergy seem to have been the least affected. Chronicles, whether of towns or of families, bear witness to the degradation of morals among the parish priests and the superior clergy. The Benedictines and their dependent Orders of monks do not appear to have shared largely in the religious movement. It was different however with the Dominicans, the Franciscans, and the mendicant Augustinians. These begging friars reformed themselves strenuously, in the medieval sense of reformation. They went back to their old lives of mortifying the flesh, of devoting themselves to works of practical benevolence and of self-denying activity. As a consequence, they, and not the parish clergy, had become the trusted religious leaders of the people. Their chapels were thronged by the common folk, and the better disposed nobles and burghers took them for their confessors and spiritual directors. It was in vain that the Roman Curia proclaimed, by its Legates in Germany, the old doctrine that the benefits of religious acts do not depend upon the personal character of the administrators; that it published regulations binding all parishioners to confess at least once a year to their parish priests. The people, high and low, felt that Bishops who rode to the Diet accompanied by their concubines disguised in men's clothing, and parish priests who were tavern-keepers or the most frequent customers at the village public-house, were not true spiritual guides. They turned for the consolations of religion to the poor-living, hard-working Franciscans and Augustinian Eremites who listened to their confessions and spoke comfortingly to their souls, who taught the children and said masses without taking fees. The last decades of the fifteenth century were the time of a revival in the spiritual power and devotion of the mendicant Orders.

One result of the underlying fear which inspired this religious revival was the way in which the personality of Christ was constantly regarded in the common Christian thought of the time as it is revealed to us in autobiographies, in sermons, and in pictorial representations. The Saviour was concealed behind the Judge, who was to come to punish the wicked. Luther tells us that when he was a boy in the parish church his childish imagination was inflamed by the stained-glass picture of Jesus, not the Saviour, but the Judge, of a fierce countenance, seated on a rainbow, and carrying a flaming sword in His hand. This idea prevented pious people who held it from approaching Jesus as an intercessor. He Himself needed to be interceded with on behalf of the poor sinners He was coming to judge. And this thought in turn gave to the adoration of the Virgin Mother a strength and intensity hitherto unknown in medieval religion. The doctrine of the Immaculate Conception had strenuous advocates; men and women formed themselves into confraternities that they might beseech her intercession with the strength that numbers give; and these confraternities spread all over Germany. The intercessory powers of the Virgin Mother became a more and more important element in the popular religion, and little books of devotion were in circulation—the *Little Gospel*, the *Pearl of the Passion*—which related with many a comment the words of Christ on the Cross to St John and to the Virgin. Then the idea grew up that the Virgin herself had to be interceded with in order to become an intercessor; and her mother, St Anne, became the object of a cult which may almost be called new. This "Cult of the Blessed Anna" rapidly extended itself in ever-widening circles until there were few districts in Germany which had not their confraternities devoted to her service. Such was the prevailing enthusiastic popular religion of the last decades of the fifteenth century—the religion which met and surrounded a sensitive boy when he left his quiet home and entered the world. It had small connexion, save in the one point of the increased reverence paid to the Virgin, with the theology of the Schools, but it was the religious force among the people.

Side by side with this flamboyant popular religion can be discerned another spiritual movement so unlike it, so utterly divergent from it in character and in aim, that it is surprising to detect its presence within the same areas and at the same period, and that we need scarcely wonder that it has been so largely overlooked. Its great characteristic was that laymen began to take into their own hands matters which had hitherto been supposed to be the exclusive property of churchmen. We can discern the impulse setting in motion at the same time princes, burghers, and artisans, each class in its own way.

The Great Council of Constance had pledged the Church to a large number of practical reforms, aiming at the reinvigoration of the various local ecclesiastical institutions. These pledges had never been fulfilled, and their non-fulfilment accounts for one side of the German opposition to Rome. During the last decades of the fifteenth century some of the German Princes assumed the right to see that within their lands proper discipline was exercised over the clergy as well as over the laity. To give instances would need more space than this chapter affords. It is enough to say that the *jus episcopale* which Luther claimed in later days for the civil power had been exercised, and that for the good of the people, in the lands of Brandenburg and of Saxony before the close of the fifteenth century. We have therefore this new thing, that the laity in power had begun to set quietly aside the immunities and privileges of the Church, to this extent at least, that the civil authorities compelled the local ecclesiastical institutions within their dominions to live under the rule of reform laid down by an ecumenical council, and that they did this despite the remonstrances of the superior ecclesiastical authorities.

The same assertion of the rights of laymen to do Christian work in their own way appears when the records of the boroughs are examined. The whole charitable system of the Middle Ages had been administered by the Church; all bequests for the relief of the poor had been placed in the hands of the clergy; and all donations for the relief of the poor were given to clerical managers. The burghers saw the charitable bequests of their forefathers grossly perverted from their original purposes, and it began to dawn upon them that, although the law of charity was part of the law of Christ, it did not necessarily follow that all charities must be under ecclesiastical administration. Hence cases appear, and that more frequently as the years pass, where burghers leave their charitable bequests to be managed by the town council or other secular authority; and this particular portion of Christian work ceased to be the exclusive possession of the clergy.

Another feature of the times was the growth of an immense number of novel religious associations or confraternities. They were not, like the praying circles of the Mystics or of the *Gottesfreunde*, strictly non-clerical or anti-clerical; they had no objection to the protection of the Church, but they had a distinctively lay character. Some of them were associations of artisans; and these were commonly called *Kalands*, because it was one of their rules to meet once a month for divine service, usually in a chapel belonging to one of the mendicant Orders. Others bore curious names, such as *St Ursula's Schifflein*, and enforced a rule that all the members must pray a certain number of times a week. Pious people frequently belonged to a number of these associations. The members united for religious purposes, generally under the auspices of the Church; but they were confraternities of laymen and women who had marked out for themselves their own course of religious duties quite independently of the Church and of its traditional ideals. Perhaps no greater contribution could be made to our knowledge of the quiet religious life at the close of the fifteenth century than to gather together in a monograph what can be known about these religious confraternities.

Such was the religious atmosphere into which Luther was born and which he breathed from his earliest days. His mother taught him the simple evangelical hymns which had fed her own spiritual growth; his father had that sturdy common-sense piety which belonged to so many of the better disposed nobles, burghers, and artisans of the time; while the fear of Jesus the Judge, who was coming to judge and punish the wicked, branded itself on his child's soul when he gazed up at the vengeful picture of our Lord. He was taught at home the Ten Commandments, the Lord's Prayer, words of Jesus from the Gospels, the Creed, such simple hymns as *Christ ist erstanden, Ein kindelein so löbelich*, and *Nun bitten wir den heiligen Geist*—all that went to make what he long afterwards called "the faith of the children." His father's strong dislike to monks and friars; the Hussite propaganda, which, in spite of all attempts at repression, had penetrated the Harz and Thuringia; the Mansfeld police regulations, with other evidence from the local chronicles, show how much the lay religion had made its way among the people. The popular revival displayed itself in the great processions and pilgrimages made to holy places in his neighbourhood—to Kyffhäuser, where there was a miraculous wooden cross, to the Bruno Chapel of Querfurt, to the old chapel at Welfesholz, and to the cloister church at Wimmelburg.

Martin Luther was born on November 10, 1483, at Eisleben, and spent his childhood in Mansfeld. His father, Hans, was a miner in the Mansfeld district, where the policy of the Counts of Mansfeld, to build and let out on hire small smelting furnaces, enabled thrifty and skilled workmen to rise in the world.

The boy grew up amidst the toilsome, grimy, often coarse surroundings of the German peasant life—protected from much that was evil by the wise severity of his parents, but sharing in its hardness, its superstitions, and its simple political and ecclesiastical ideas; as that the Emperor was God's ruler on the earth who would protect poor people from the Turk; that the Church was the "Pope's house," in which the Bishop of Rome was the house-father; and that obedience and reverence were due to the lords of the soil. He went to the village school in Mansfeld and endured the cruelties of a merciless pedagogue; he was sent later to a school at Magdeburg, and then to St George's High School at Eisenach. In these boyish days he was a "poor student," *i.e.* one who got his education and lodging free, was obliged to sing in the church choir, and was permitted to sing in the streets, begging for bread. His later writings abound in references to these early school-days and to his own quiet thoughts; and they make it plain that the religion of fear was laying hold on him and driving out the earlier simple family faith. Two pictures branded themselves on his childish mind at Magdeburg. He saw a young Prince of Anhalt, who had forsaken rank and inheritance and, to save his soul, had become a barefooted friar, carrying the huge begging-sack, and worn to skin and bone by his scourgings and fastings and prayers. The other was an altar-piece in a church, the picture of a ship in which was no layman, not even a King or a Prince; in it were the Pope with his Cardinals and Bishops, and the Holy Ghost hovered over them directing their course, while priests and monks managed the oars and the sails, and thus they went sailing heavenwards. The laymen were swimming in the water beside the ship; some were drowning, others were holding on by ropes which the monks and priests cast out to them to aid them. No layman was in the ship and no ecclesiastic was in the water. The picture haunted him for years. At Eisenach he had some glimpses of the old simple family life, this time accompanied by a new refinement, in the house of the lady whom most biographers identify with Frau Cotta. But the religious atmosphere of the town which the boy inhaled and enjoyed was new. The town was under the spell of St Elizabeth, the pious Landgravine who had given up family life, children, and all earthly comforts, to earn a medieval saintship. Her good deeds were blazoned on the windows of the church in which Luther sang as choir-boy, and he had long conversations with some of the monks who belonged to her foundations. The novel surroundings tended to lead him far from the homely piety of his parents and from the more cultured family religion of his new friends, and he confesses that it was with incredulous surprise that he heard Frau Cotta say that there was nothing on earth more lovely than the love of husband and wife when it is in the fear of the Lord. He had surrendered himself to that revival of crude medieval religion which was based on fear, and which found an outlet in fastings, scourgings, pilgrimages, saint-worship, and in general in the thought that salvation demanded the abandonment of family, friends, and the activities and enjoyments of life in the world.

After three happy years at Eisenach Luther was sent to Erfurt and entered his name on the matriculation roll in letters which can still be read, Martinus Ludher ex Mansfeldt. Hans Luther had been prospering; he was able to pay for his son's college expenses; Luther was no longer a "poor student," but was able to give undivided attention to his studies. The father meant the son to become a trained lawyer; and the lad of seventeen seems to have accepted without question the career marked out for him.

The University of Erfurt was in Luther's days the most famous in Germany. It had been founded in 1392 by the burghers, and academic and burgher life mingled there as nowhere else. The graduation days were town holidays, and the graduation ceremonies always included a procession of the University authorities, the gilds and the town officials, with all the attendant medieval pomp, and concluded with a torchlight march at night. But if the University was strictly allied to the town it was as strongly united to the Church. It had been enriched with numerous papal privileges; its chancellor was the Archbishop of Mainz; many of its theological professors held ecclesiastical prebends, and others were monks of different Orders and notably of the Augustinian Eremites. The whole teaching staff went solemnly to hear mass at the beginning of every term; each faculty was under the protection of a patron Saint—St George presiding over the faculty of Philosophy; the professors had to swear to teach nothing opposed to the doctrine of the Roman Church; and care was taken to prevent the beginnings and spread of heretical opinions.

The University teaching was medieval in all essentials, but represented the new, as Cologne championed the old, scholasticism. Gabriel Biel, the disciple of William of Ockham, had been one of the teachers. Humanism of the German type, which was very different from the Italian, had found an entrance as early as 1460 in the persons of Peter Luder and Jacob Publicius, and in the following years there was a good deal of intercourse between Erfurt scholars and Italian humanists. Maternus Pistoris was lecturing on the Latin classics in 1494 and had for his colleague Nicholas Marschalk, who was the first to establish a printing-press in Germany for Greek books. They had speedily gathered round them a band of enthusiastic scholars, Johannes Jäger of Dornheim (Crotus Rubeanus), Henry and Peter Eberbach, George Burkhardt of Spalt (Spalatinus), John Lange, and others known afterwards in the earlier stages of the Reformation movement. Conrad Muth (Mutianus Rufus), who had studied in Italy, was one of the leaders; Eoban of Hesse (Helius Eobanus Hessus), perhaps the most gifted of them all, joined the circle in 1494. These humanists did not attack openly the older course of study at Erfurt. They wrote complimentary Latin poems in praise of their older colleagues; they formed a select circle who were called the "Poets"; they affected to correspond with each other after the manner of the ancients. In private, Mutianus and Crotus seem to have delighted to reveal their eclectic theosophy to a band of half-terrified, half-admiring youths; to say that there was but one God, who had the various names of Jupiter, Mars, Hercules, Jesus, and one Goddess, who was called Juno, Diana, or Mary as the worshippers chose; but these things were not supposed to be for the public ear.

The University of Erfurt in the beginning of the sixteenth century was the recognised meeting-place of the two opposing tendencies of scholasticism and humanism; and it was also, perhaps in a higher degree than any other university, a place where the student was exposed to many other diverse influences. The system of biblical exegesis first stimulated by Nicholas de Lyra, which cannot be classed under scholasticism or humanism, had found a succession of able teachers in Erfurt. The strong anti-clerical teaching of Jacob of Jüterbogk and of John Wessel, who had taught in Erfurt for fifteen years, had left its mark on the University and was not forgotten. Low mutterings of the Hussite propaganda itself, Luther tells us, could be heard from time to time, urging a strange Christian socialism which was at the same time thoroughly anti-clerical. Then over against all this opportunities were occasionally given, at the visits of papal Legates, for seeing the magnificence and might of the Roman Church and of the Pope its head. In 1502 and again in 1504, during Luther's student days, Cardinal Raimund, sent to proclaim in Germany new and unheard-of Indulgences, visited the university town. The civic dignitaries, the Rector Magnificus with the whole University, all the clergy, the monks and the school children, accompanied by crowds of the townsfolk, went out in procession to meet him and escort him with due ceremony into the city. Add to this the gross dissipation existing among many of the student sets, and the whisperings of foul living on the part of many of the higher clergy in the town, and some idea can be formed of the sea of trouble, doubt, questioning, and anxiety into which a bright, sensitive, imaginative, and piously disposed lad of seventeen was thrown when he had begun his student life in Erfurt.

When we piece together references in correspondence to Luther's student life, recollections of his fellow-students, and scattered sayings of his own in after-life, we get upon the whole the idea of a very levelheaded youth, with a strong sense of the practical side of his studies, thoroughly respected by his professors, refusing to be carried away into any excess of humanist enthusiasm on the one hand or of physical dissipation on the other; intent only to profit by the educational advantages within his reach and to justify the sacrifices which his father was making on his behalf. He had been sent to Erfurt to become a jurist, and the faculty of Philosophy afforded the preparation for the faculty of Law as well as of Theology. Luther accordingly began the course of study prescribed in the faculty of Philosophy— Logic, Dialectic, and Rhetoric, followed by Physics and Astronomy, the teaching in all cases consisting of abstract classification and distinctions without any real study of life or of fact. The teacher he most esteemed was Jodocus Trutvetter, the famed "Erfurt Doctor" whose fame and genius, as all good Germans thought, had made Erfurt as well-known as Paris. Scholasticism, he said, left him little time for poetry and classical studies. He does not seem to have attended any of the humanist lectures. But he read privately a large number of the Latin classical authors. Virgil, whose pages he opened with some dread,—for was he not in medieval popular legend a combination of wizard and prophet of Christ?—became his favourite author. His peasant upbringing made him take great delight in the *Bucolics* and *Georgics*—books, he said, that only a herd and a countryman can rightly understand. Cicero charmed him; he delighted in his public labours for his country and in his versatility, and believed him to be a much better philosopher than Aristotle. He read Livy, Terence, and Plautus. He prized the pathetic portions of Horace but esteemed him inferior to Prudentius. He seems also to have read from a volume of selections portions of Propertius, Persius, Lucretius, Tibullus, Silvius Italicus, Statius, and Claudian. We hear of him studying Greek privately with John Lange. But he was never a member of the humanist circle, and in his student days was personally unacquainted with its leading members. He had none of the humanist enthusiasm for the language and the spirit of the past; what he cared for was the knowledge of human life which classical authors gave him. Besides, the "epicurean" life and ideas of the young humanist circle displeased him. They, on their part, would evidently have received him gladly. They called him "the philosopher," they spoke about his gifts of singing and lute-playing, and of his frank, engaging character. In later days he could make use of humanism; but he never was a humanist in spirit or in aim. He was too much in earnest about religious matters, and of too practical a turn of mind.

Luther's course of study flowed on regularly. He was a bright, sociable, hard-working student and took his various degrees in an exceptionally short time. He was Bachelor in 1502, and Master in 1505, when he stood second among the seventeen successful candidates. He had attained what he had once thought the summit of earthly felicity and found himself marching in a procession of University magnates and civic dignitaries clothed in his new robes. His father, proud of his son's success, sent him the costly present of a *Corpus Juris*. He may have begun to attend lectures in the faculty of Law, when he suddenly retired into a convent and became a monk.

This action was so unexpected that his student friends made all sorts of conjectures about his reasons, and these have been woven into stories which are pure legends. Little or nothing is known about Luther's religious convictions during his stay at Erfurt. This is the more surprising since Luther was the least reticent of men. His correspondence, his sermons, his commentaries, all his books are full of little autobiographical details. He tells what he felt when a child, what his religious thoughts were during his school-days; but he is silent about his thoughts and feelings during his years at Erfurt, and especially during the months which preceded his plunge into the convent. He has himself made two statements about his resolve to become a monk, and they comprise the only accurate information obtainable. He says that the resolve was sudden, and that he left the world and entered the cloister because "he doubted of himself"; that in his case the proverb was true, "doubt makes a monk."

What was the doubting? The modern mind is tempted to imagine intellectual difficulties, to think of the rents in the Church's theology which the criticisms of Ockham and of Biel had produced, of the complete antagonism between the whole ecclesiastical mode of thinking and the enlightenment from ancient culture that humanism was producing, and Luther's doubtings are frequently set down to the self-questioning which his contact with humanism in Erfurt had produced. But this idea, if not foreign to the age, was strange to Luther. He doubted whether he could ever do what he thought had to be done by him to save his soul if he remained in the world. That was what compelled him to enter the convent. The lurid fires of Hell and the pale shades of purgatory which are the constant background to Dante's Paradise were always present to the mind of Luther from boyhood. Could he escape the one and win the other if he remained in the world? He doubted it and entered the convent.

The Order of monks which Luther selected was the Augustinian Eremites. Their history was somewhat curious. Originally they had been formed out of the numerous hermits who lived solitary religious lives throughout Italy and Germany. Several Popes had desired to bring them together into convents; and this was at last effected by Alexander IV, who had enjoined them to frame their constitution according to the Rule of St Augustine. No other order of monks shared so largely in the religious revival of the fifteenth century. The convents which had reformed associated themselves together into what was called the Congregation. The reformed Augustinian Eremites strictly observed their vows of poverty and obedience; they led self-denying lives; they represented the best type of later medieval piety. Their convents were for the most part in the larger towns of Germany, and the monks were generally held in high esteem by the citizens who took them for confessors and spiritual directors. The Brethren were encouraged to study, and this was done so successfully that professorships in theology and in philosophy in most of the Universities of Germany in the fifteenth century were filled by Augustinian Eremites. They also cultivated the art of preaching; most of the larger convents had a special preacher attached; and the townspeople flocked to hear him.

Their theology had little to do with Augustine; nor does Luther appear to have studied Augustine until he had removed to Wittenberg. Their views belonged to the opposite pole of medieval thought and closely resembled those of the Franciscans. No Order paid more reverence to the Blessed Virgin. Her image stood in the Chapter-house of every convent; their theologians were strenuous defenders of the Immaculate Conception; they aided to spread the "cult of the Blessed Anna." They were strong advocates of papal supremacy. In the person of John von Palz, the professor of theology in the Erfurt convent and the teacher of Luther himself, they furnished the most outspoken defender of papal Indulgences. This was the Order into which Luther so suddenly threw himself in 1505.

He spent the usual year as a novice, then took the vows, and was set to study theology. His text-books were the writings of Occam, Biel, and D'Ailly. His aptness for study, his vigour and precision in debate, his acumen, excited the admiration of his teachers. But Luther had not come to the convent to study theology; he had entered to save his soul. These studies were but pastime; his serious and dominating task was to win the sense of pardon of sin and to see his body a temple of the Holy Ghost. He fasted and prayed and scourged himself according to rule, and invented additional methods of maceration. He edified his brethren; they spoke of him as a model of monastic piety; but the young man—he was only twenty-three—felt no relief and was no nearer God. He was still tormented by the sense of sin which urged him to repeated confession. God was always the implacable judge inexorably threatening punishment for the guilt of breaking a law which it seemed impossible to keep. For it was the righteousness of God that terrified him; the thought that all his actions were tested by the standard of that righteousness of God. His superiors could not understand him. Staupitz, Vicar-General of the Order, saw him on one of his visitations and was attracted by him. He saw his sincerity, his deep trouble, his hopeless despair. He advised him to study the Bible, St Augustine, and Tauler. An old monk helped him for a short time by explaining that the Creed taught the forgiveness of sin as a promise of God, and that what the sinner had to do was to trust in the promise. But the thought would come: Pardon follows contrition and confession; how can I know that my contrition has gone deep enough; how can I be sure that my confession has been complete? At last Staupitz began to see where the difficulty lay, and made suggestions which helped him. The true mission of the medieval Church had been to be a stern preacher of righteousness. It taught, and elevated its rude converts, by placing before them ideals of saintly piety and of ineffable purity, and by teaching them that sin was sin in spite of extenuating circumstances. Luther was a true son of that medieval Church. Her message had sunk deeply into his soul; it had been enforced by his experience of the popular revival of the decades which had preceded and followed his birth. He felt more deeply than most the point where it failed. It contrasted the Divine righteousness and man's sin and weakness. It insisted on the inexorable demands of the law of God and at the same time pronounced despairingly that man could never fulfil them. Staupitz showed Luther that the antinomy had been created by setting over against each other the righteousness of God and the sin and helplessness of man, and by keeping these two thoughts in opposition; then he explained that the righteousness of God, according to God's promise, might become the possession of man in and through Christ. Fellowship of man with God solved the antinomy; all fellowship is founded on personal trust; and faith gives man that fellowship with God through which all things that belong to God can become his. These thoughts, acted upon, helped Luther gradually to win his way to peace of heart. Penitence and confession, which had been the occasions of despair when extorted by fear, became natural and spontaneous when suggested by a sense of the greatness and intimacy of the redeeming love of God in Christ.

The intensity and sincerity of this protracted struggle marked Luther for life. It gave him a strength of character and a living power which never left him. The end of the long inner fight had freed him from the burden which had oppressed him, and his naturally frank, joyous nature found a free outlet. It gave him a sense of freedom, and the feeling that life was something given by God to be enjoyed,—the same feeling that humanism, from its lower level, had given to so many of its disciples. For the moment however nothing seemed questionable. He was a faithful son of the Medieval Church, "the Pope's house," with its Cardinals and its Bishops, its priests, monks, and nuns, its masses and its relics, its Indulgences and its pilgrimages. All these external things remained unchanged. The one thing that was changed was the relation in which one human soul stood to God. He was still a monk who believed in his vocation. The very fact that his conversion had come to him within the convent made him the more sure that he had done right to take the monastic vow.

Soon after he had attained inward peace Luther was ordained, and Hans Luther came from Mansfeld for the ceremony, not that he took any pleasure in it, but because he did not wish to shame his eldest son. The sturdy peasant adhered to his anti-clerical Christianity, and when his son told him that he had a clear call from God to the monastic life, the father suggested that it might have been a prompting from the devil. Once ordained, it was Luther's duty to say mass and to hear confessions, impose penance and pronounce absolution. He had no difficulties about the doctrines and usages of the Church; but he put his own meaning into the duties and position of a confessor. His own experience had taught him that man could never forgive sin; that belonged to God alone. But the human confessor could be the spiritual guide of those who came to confess to him; he could warn them against false grounds of confidence, and show them the pardoning grace of God.

Luther's theological studies were continued. He devoted himself to Augustine, to Bernard, to men who might be called " experimental " theologians. He began to show himself a good man of business, with an eye for the heart of things. Staupitz and his chiefs entrusted him with some delicate commissions on behalf of the Order, and made quiet preparation for his advancement. In 1508 he, with a few other brother monks, was transferred from the convent at Erfurt to that at Wittenberg, to assist the small University there.

Some years before this the Elector Frederick the Wise of Saxony, the head of the Ernestine branch of his House, had resolved to provide a university for his own dominions. He had been much drawn to the Augustinian Eremites since his first acquaintance with them at Grimma when he was a boy at school. Naturally Staupitz became his chief adviser in his new scheme; indeed the University from the first might almost be called an educational establishment belonging to the

Augustinian Eremites. There was not much money to spare at the Electoral Court. A sum got from the sale of Indulgences some years before, which Frederick had not allowed to leave the country, served to make a beginning. Prebends attached to the Castle Church—the Church of All Saints was its ecclesiastical name—furnished the salaries of some of the professors; the other teachers were to be supplied from the monks of the convent of the Augustinian Eremites in the town. The Emperor Maximilian granted the usual imperial privileges, and the University was opened October 18, 1502. Staupitz himself was one of the professors and dean of the faculty of Theology; another Augustinian Eremite was dean of the faculty of Arts. The patron Saints of the Order, the Blessed Virgin and St Augustine, were the patron Saints of the University. Some distinguished teachers, outside the Augustinian Eremites, were induced to come, among others Jerome Schurf from Tübingen; Staupitz collected promising young monks from convents of his Order and enrolled them as students; other youths were attracted by the teachers and came from various parts of Germany. The University enrolled 416 students during its first year. This success, however, appears to have been artificial; the numbers gradually declined to 56 in the summer session of 1505. The first teachers left it for more promising places. Still Staupitz encouraged Frederick to persevere. New teachers were secured—among them Nicholas Amsdorf, who had then a great reputation as a teacher of the old-fashioned scholasticism, and Andrew Bodenstein of Carlstadt. The University began to grow slowly.

Luther was sent to Wittenberg in 1508. He was made to teach the Dialectic and Physics of Aristotle, a task which he disliked, but whether in the University or to the young monks in the convent it is impossible to say. He also began to preach. His work was interrupted by a command to go to Rome on the business of his Order. The Augustinian Eremites, as has been already said, were divided into the unreformed and the reformed convents—the latter being united in an association which was called the Congregation. Staupitz was anxious to heal this schism and to bring all the convents in Germany within the reformation. Difficulties arose, and the interests of peace demanded that both the General of the Order and the Curia should be informed on all the circumstances. A messenger was needed, one whom he could trust and who would also be trusted by the stricter party among his monks. No one seemed more suitable than the young monk Martin Luther.

Luther saw Rome, and the impressions made upon him by his visit remained with him all his life. He and his companion approached the imperial city with the liveliest expectations; but they were the longings of the pious pilgrim, not those of the scholar of the Renaissance—so little impression had humanism made upon him. When he first caught sight of the city Luther raised his hands in an ecstasy, exclaiming, "I greet thee, thou Holy Rome, thrice holy from the blood of the Martyrs." That was his mood of mind—so little had his convent struggles and the peace he had found in the thought that the just live by faith separated him from the religious ideas of his time.

His official business did not cost much time; he seems to have had no complaints to make against the Curia; indeed the business on which he had been sent seems to have been settled in Germany by an amicable compromise. His official work done, he set himself to see the Holy City with the devotion of a pilgrim and the thoroughness of a German. He visited all the shrines, especially those to which Indulgences were attached. He climbed the thirty-eight steps which led to the vestibule of St Peter's—every step counting seven years' remission of penance; he knelt before all the altars; he listened reverently to all the accounts given him of the various relics and believed them all; he thought that if his parents had been dead, he could, by saying masses in certain chapels, secure them against purgatory. He visited the remains of antiquity which could tell him something of the life of the old Romans —the Pantheon, the Coliseum, and the Baths of Diocletian.

But if Luther was still unemancipated from his belief in relics, in the effect of pilgrimages, and in the validity of Indulgences for the remission of imposed penance, his sturdy German piety and his plain Christian morality turned his reverence of Rome into a loathing. The city he had greeted as holy, he found to be a sink of iniquity; its very priests were infidel, and openly scoffed at the sacred services they performed; the papal courtiers were men of depraved lives; the Cardinals of the Church lived in open sin; he had frequent cause to repeat the Italian proverb, first spread abroad by Machiavelli and by Bembo, "The nearer Rome the worse Christian." It meant much for him in after-days that he had seen Rome for himself.

Luther was back in Wittenberg early in the summer of 1512. Staupitz sent him to Erfurt to complete the steps necessary for the higher graduation in Theology, preparatory to succeeding Staupitz in the Chair of Theology in Wittenberg. He graduated as Doctor of the Holy Scripture, took the Wittenberg doctor's oath to defend evangelical truth vigorously (*viriliter*), was made a member of the Senate three days later, and a few weeks after he succeeded Staupitz as Professor of Theology.

From the first Luther's lectures differed from what were then expected from a professor of theology. It was not that he criticised the theology then current in the Church; he had an entirely different idea of what theology ought to be, and of what it ought to make known. His whole habit of mind was practical, and theology for him was an "experimental" discipline. It ought to be, he thought, a study which would teach how a man could find the grace of God, and, having found it, how he could persevere in a life of joyous obedience to God and His commandments. He had, himself, sought, and that with deadly earnest, an answer to this question in all the material which the Church of the time had accumulated to aid men in the task. He had tried to find it in the penitential system, in the means of grace, in theology professedly based on Holy Scripture expounded by the later Schoolmen and Mystics, and his search had been in vain. But theologians like Bernard and Augustine had helped him, and as they had taught him he could teach others. That was the work he set himself to do. It was a task to which contemporary theology had not given any special prominence, and which, in Luther's opinion, it had ignored. His theology was new, because in his opinion it ought to be occupied with a new task, not because the conclusions reached by contemporary theology occupied with other tasks were necessarily wrong.

Luther never knew much Hebrew, and he used the Vulgate in his prelections. He had a huge, widely printed volume on his desk, and wrote the heads of his lectures between the printed lines. The pages still exist and can be studied. We can trace the gradual growth of his theology. In the years 1513–15 there is no sign of any attack upon the contemporary Scholastic teaching, no thought but that the monastic life is the flower of Christian piety. He expounded the Psalms; his aids are what are called the mystical passages in St Augustine and in Bernard, but what may be more properly termed those portions of their teaching in which they insist upon and describe personal religion. These thoughts simply push aside the ordinary theology of the day without staying to criticise it. We can discern in the germ what grew to be the main thoughts in the later Lutheran theology. Men are redeemed apart from any merits of their own; man's faith is trust in the verity of God and in the historical work of Christ. These thoughts were for the most part expressed in the formulae common to the scholastic philosophy of the time; but they grew in clearness of expression, and took shape as a series of propositions which formed the basis of his teaching—that man wins pardon through the free grace of God, that when man lays hold on God's promise of pardon he becomes a new creature, that this sense of pardon is the beginning of a new life of sanctification. To these may be added the thoughts that the life of faith is Christianity on its inward side; that the contrast between the economy of law and that of grace is something fundamental; and that there is a real distinction to be drawn between the outward and visible Church and the ideal Church, which is to be described by its spiritual and moral relations to God after the manner of Augustine. The years 1515 and 1516 give traces of a more thorough study of Augustine and of the German Mystics. This comes out in the college lectures on the Epistle to the Romans and in some minor publications. His language loses its scholastic colouring and adopts many of the well-known mystical phrases, especially when he describes the natural incapacity of men for what is good. Along with this change in language, and evidently related to it, we find evidence that Luther was beginning to think less highly of the monastic life and its external renunciations. Predestination, meaning by that not an abstract metaphysical dogma, but the thought that the whole of the believer's life and what it involved depended in the last resort on God and not on man, came more and more into the foreground. Still there did not appear any disposition to criticise or repudiate the current theology of the day.

But about the middle of 1516 Luther had reached the parting of the ways, and the divergence appeared on the practical and not on the speculative side of theology. It began in a sermon he preached on the theory of Indulgences in July, 1516, and increased month by month—the widening divergence can be clearly traced step by step—until he could contrast "our theology," the theology taught by Luther and his colleagues at Wittenberg, with what was taught elsewhere and notably at Erfurt. The former represented Augustine and the Bible; the latter was founded on Aristotle. In September, 1517, his position had become so clear that he wrote against the scholastic theology, declaring that it was at heart Pelagian and that it obscured and buried out of sight the Augustinian doctrines of grace. He bewailed the fact that the current theology neglected to teach the supreme value of faith and of inward righteousness, that it encouraged men to seek to escape the due reward of sin by means of Indulgences, instead of exhorting them to practise that inward repentance which belongs to every genuine Christian life. It was at this stage of his own inward religious development that Luther felt himself forced to stand forth in public in opposition to the sale of Indulgences in Germany.

Luther had become much more than a professor of theology by this time. He had become a power in Wittenberg. His lectures seemed like a revelation of the Scriptures to the Wittenberg students; grave burghers from the town matriculated at the University in order to attend his classes; his fame gradually spread, and students began to flock from all parts of Germany to the small, poor, and remote town; and the Elector grew proud of his University and of the man who had given it such a position. In these earlier years of his professoriate Luther undertook the duties of the preacher in the town church in Wittenberg. He became a great preacher, able to touch the conscience and bring men to amend their lives. Like all great preachers of the day who were in earnest he denounced prevalent sins; he deplored the low standard set by the leaders of the Church in principle and in practice; he declared that religion was not an easy thing; that it did not consist in externals; that both sin and true repentance had their roots in the heart; and that until the heart had been made pure all kinds of external purifications were useless. Such a man, occupying the position he had won, could not keep silent when he saw what he believed to be a great source of moral corruption gathering round him and infecting the people whom he taught daily, and who had selected him as their confessor and the religious guide of their lives.

Luther began his work as a Reformer in an attack on what was called an Indulgence proclaimed in 1513 by Pope Leo X, farmed by Albert of Brandenburg, Archbishop of Mainz, and preached by John Tetzel, a Dominican monk who had been commissioned by Albert to sell for him the "papal letters," as the Indulgence tickets were called. The money raised was to be devoted to the building of St Peter's Church in Rome, and to raise a tomb worthy of the great Apostle who, it was said, lay in a Roman grave. People had come to be rather sceptical about the destination of moneys raised by Indulgences; but the buyers had their "papal letters," and it did not much matter to them where the money went after it had left their pockets. The seller of Indulgences had generally a magnificent welcome when he entered a German town. He drew near it in the centre of a procession with the Bull announcing the Indulgence, carried before him on a cloth of gold and velvet, and all the priests and monks of the town, the Burgomaster and Town Council, the teachers and the school-children and a crowd of citizens went out to meet him with banners and lighted candles, and escorted him into the town singing hymns. When the gates were reached all the bells began to ring, the church-organs were played, the crowd, with the commissary in their midst, streamed into the principal church, where a great red cross was erected and the Pope's banner displayed. Then followed sermons and speeches by the commissary and his attendants extolling the Indulgence, narrating its wonderful virtues, and inviting the people to buy. The Elector of Saxony had refused to allow the commissary to enter his territories; but the commissary could approach most parts of the Elector's dominions without actually crossing the boundaries. Tetzel had come to Jüterbogk in Magdeburg territory and Zerbst in Anhalt, and had opened the sale of Indulgences there; and people from Wittenberg had gone to these places and made purchases. They had brought their "papal letters" to Luther and had demanded that he should acknowledge their efficacy. He had refused; the buyers had complained to Tetzel and the commissary had uttered threats; Luther felt himself in great perplexity. The Indulgence, and the addresses by which it was commended, he knew, were doing harm to poor souls; he got the letter of instructions given to Tetzel by his employer, the Archbishop of Mainz, and his heart waxed wroth against it. Still at the basis of the Indulgence, bad as it was, Luther thought that there was a great truth; that it is the business of the Church to declare the free and sovereign grace of God apart from all human satisfactions.

The practice of Indulgences was, in his days, universal and permeated the whole Church life of the times. A large number of the pious associations among laymen, which formed so marked a feature of the fifteenth century piety, were founded on ideas that lay at the basis of the practice of granting Indulgences. Pious Christians of the fifteenth century accepted the religious machinery of their Church as unquestioningly and as quietly as they did the laws of nature. That machinery included among other things an inexhaustible treasury of good works— of prayers, fastings, mortifications of all kinds—which holy men and women had done, and which might be of service to others, if the Pope could only be persuaded to transfer them. When a pious confraternity was formed, the Pope, it was believed, could transfer to the credit of the community a mass of prayers, almsgivings, and other ecclesiastical good deeds, all of which became for the members of the confraternity what a bank advance is to a man starting in business. Some of these associations bought their spiritual treasure from the Pope for so much cash, but there was not always any buying or selling. There was none in the celebrated association of *St Ursula's Schifflein*, to which so many devout people, the Elector himself included, belonged. Probably little paying of cash took place in the thirty-two pious confraternities of which Dr Pfeffinger, the trusted Councillor of the Elector Frederick, was a member. The machinery of the Church, however, secured this advantage that, if by any accident the members of the association failed in praying as they had promised, they had always this transferred treasure to fall back upon. There could be little difference in principle between the Pope transferring a mass of spiritual benefits to a pious brotherhood, and his handing over an indefinite amount to the Archbishop of Mainz to be disposed of, as the prelate thought fit, through Tetzel or others.

Moreover, it must be remembered that in the course of Luther's religious life down to 1517 there are no traces of anything quixotic; and that is a wonderful proof of the simplicity and strength of his character. He had something of a contempt for men who believe that they are born to set the world right; he compared them to a player at ninepins who imagines he can knock down twelve pins when there are only nine standing. It was only after much hesitation and deep distress of mind that he felt compelled to interfere, and it was his intense earnestness in the practical moral life of his townsmen that compelled him to step forward. When he did intervene he went about the matter with a mixture of prudence and courage which were eminently characteristic of the man.

The Castle Church of Wittenberg had always been closely connected with the University, and its doors had been used for publication of important academic documents; notices of public disputations on theological matters, common enough at the time, had doubtless often been seen figuring there. The day of the year which drew the largest concourse of townsmen and strangers to the church was the first of

November, All Saints' Day. It was the anniversary of the consecration of the church, was commemorated by a prolonged series of services, and the benefits of an Indulgence were secured to all who took part in them. At noon on All Saints' Day, Luther nailed his Ninety-five Theses to the door of the church. It was an academic proceeding. A doctor in theology offered to hold a disputation, such was the usual term, for the purpose of explaining the efficacy of the Indulgence. The explanation had ninety-five heads or propositions, all of which "Doctor Martin Luther, theologian," offered to make good against all comers. The subject, judged by the numberless books which had been written upon it, was eminently suitable for debate; the propositions offered were to be matters of discussion; and the author was not supposed, according to the usage of the times, to be definitely committed to the opinions he had expressed; they were simply heads of debate. The document differed however from most academic disputations in this that everyone wished to read it. A duplicate was made in German. Copies of the Latin original and of the German translation were sent to the University printing-house and the presses there could not throw them off fast enough to meet the demand which came from all parts of Germany.

The question which Luther raised in his theses was a difficult one; the theological doctrine of Indulgences was one of the most complicated of the times, and ecclesiastical opinion on many of the points involved was doubtful. It was part of the penitential system of the medieval Church, and had changed from time to time according to the changes in that system. Indeed it may be said that in the matter of Indulgences doctrine had always been framed to justify practices and changes in practice. The beginnings go back a thousand years before the time of Luther.

In the ancient Church serious sins involved separation from the fellowship of Christians, and readmission to the communion was dependent not merely on public confession but also on the manifestation of a true repentance by the performance of certain *satisfactions*, such as the manumission of slaves, prolonged fastings, extensive almsgiving; which were supposed to be well-pleasing in God's sight, and were also the warrant for the community that the penitent might be again received within their midst. It often happened that these satisfactions were mitigated; penitents might fall sick and the prescribed fasting could not be insisted upon without danger of death—in which case the impossible satisfaction could be exchanged for an easier one, or the community might be convinced of the sincerity of the repentance without insisting that the prescribed satisfaction should be fully performed. These exchanges and mitigations are the germs out of which Indulgences grew.

In course of time the public confessions became private confessions made to a priest, and the satisfactions private satisfactions imposed by the confessor. This change involved among other things a wider circle of sins to be confessed—sins of thought, the sources of sinful actions, brought to light by the confessor's questions; and different satisfactions were imposed at the discretion of the priest corresponding to the sins confessed. This led to the construction of penitentiaries containing lists of penances supposed to be proportionate to the sins. In many cases the penances were very severe and extended over a long course of years. From the seventh century there arose a system of commutations of penances. A penance of several years' practice of fasting might be commuted into saying so many prayers or psalms, giving prescribed alms or even into a money fine—and in this last case the analogy of the *Wergeld* of the Germanic codes was frequently followed. This new custom commonly took the form that anyone who visited a prescribed church on a day that was named and gave a contribution to the funds of the church had his penance shortened by one-seventh, one-third, one-half, as the case might be. This was in every case a commutation of a penance which had been imposed according to the regulations of the Church (*relaxatio de injuncta poenitentiâ*). This power of commuting imposed penance was usually supposed to be in the hands of Bishops, and was used by them to provide funds for the building of their great churches. But priests for a time also thought themselves entitled to follow the episcopal example; and did so until the great abuse of the system made the Church insist that the power should be strictly kept in episcopal hands. Thus the real origin of Indulgences is to be found in the relaxation by the Church of a portion of the ecclesiastical penalties imposed according to regular custom.

Three conceptions, however, combined to effect a series of changes in the character of Indulgences, all of which were in operation in the beginning of the thirteenth century. These were the formulation of the thought of a Treasury of merits, the change of the institution of penance into the Sacrament of Penance, and the distinction between attrition and contrition. The two former led to the belief that the Pope alone had the power to grant Indulgences—the treasure needed a guardian to prevent its being squandered; and, when Indulgences were judged to be extra-sacramental and a matter of jurisdiction and not of Orders, they belonged to the Pope, whose jurisdiction was supreme.

The conception of a Treasury of merits was first formulated by Alexander of Hales in the thirteenth century, and his ideas were accepted and stated with more precision by the great Schoolmen who followed him. Starting with the existing practice in the Church that some penances, such for example as pilgrimages, might be performed vicariously, and bringing together the conceptions that all the faithful are one community, that the good deeds of all the members are the common property of all, that sinners may benefit by the good deeds of their fellows, that the sacrifice of Christ is sufficient to wipe out the sins of all, theologians gradually formulated the doctrine that there was a common storehouse containing the good deeds of living men, of the saints in heaven, and the inexhaustible merits of Christ, and that the merits there accumulated had been placed in the charge of the Pope and could be dispensed by him to the faithful. The doctrine was not thoroughly defined in the fifteenth century, but it was generally accepted and increased the power and resources of the Pope. It had one immediate consequence on the theory of Indulgences. They were no longer regarded as the substitution of some enjoined work for a canonical penance; they could be looked upon as an absolute equivalent of what was due to God, paid over to Him out of this Treasury of merits.

When the institution became the Sacrament of Penance it was divided into three parts—Contrition, Confession, and Satisfaction; and Absolution was made to accompany Confession and therefore to precede Satisfaction, which it had formerly followed. Satisfaction lost its old meaning. It was not the outward sign of inward sorrow, the test of fitness for pardon, and the necessary precedent of Absolution. According to the new theory, Absolution, which followed Confession and preceded Satisfaction, had the effect of removing the whole guilt of the sins confessed, and, with the guilt, the whole of the eternal punishment due; but this cancelling of guilt and of eternal punishment did not open straightway the gates of Heaven. It was thought that the Divine righteousness could not permit the baptised sinner to escape all punishment; so the idea of temporal punishment was introduced, and these *poenae temporales*, strictly distinguished from the eternal, included punishment in Purgatory. The pains of Purgatory therefore were not included in the Absolution, and everyone must suffer these had not God in His mercy provided an alternative in temporal Satisfactions. This gave rise to a great uncertainty; for who could have the assurance that the priest in imposing the Satisfaction or penance had calculated rightly and had assigned the equivalent which the righteousness of God demanded? It was here that the new idea of Indulgences came in to aid the faithful. Indulgences in the sense of relaxations of imposed penance went into the background, and the valuable Indulgence was what would secure against the pains of Purgatory. Thus in the opinion of Alexander of Hales, of Bonaventura, and above all of Thomas Aquinas, the real value of Indulgences is that they procure the remission of penalties after Contrition, Confession, and Absolution, whether these penalties have been imposed by the priest or not; and when the uncertainty of the imposed penalties is considered, Indulgences are most valuable with regard to the unimposed penalties; the priest might make a mistake, but God does not.

While, as has been seen, Indulgences were always related to Satisfactions and changed in character with the changes introduced into the meaning of these, they were not less closely affected by the distinction which came to be drawn between Attrition and Contrition. Until the thirteenth century it was always held that Contrition or a condition of real sorrow for sin was the one thing taken into account in the according of pardon to the sinner. The theologians of that century however began to make a distinction between Contrition, or godly sorrow, and Attrition, a certain amount of sorrow which might arise from a variety of causes of a more or less unworthy nature. It was held that this Attrition, though of itself too imperfect to win the pardon of God, could become perfected through the Confession heard by the priest and the Absolution administered by him. When this idea was placed in line with the thoughts developed as to the nature of the Sacrament of Penance, it followed that the weaker the form of sorrow and the greater the sins confessed and absolved, the heavier were the temporal penalties demanded by the righteousness of God. Indulgences appealed strongly to the indifferent Christian who knew that he had sinned, and who knew at the same time that his sorrow did not amount to Contrition. His conscience, however weak, told him that he could not sin with perfect impunity and that something more was needed than his perfunctory confession and the absolution of the priest. He felt that he must make some amends; that he must perform some satisfying act, or obtain an Indulgence at some cost to himself. Hence, for the ordinary indifferent Christian Attrition, Confession, and Indulgence, stood forth as the three great heads of the scheme of the Church for his salvation.

This doctrine of Attrition and its applications had not the undivided support of the Church of the later Middle Ages, but it was the doctrine which was taught by most of the Scotist divines who took the lead in theological thinking during these times. It was taught in its most pronounced form by such a representative man as John von Palz, who was professor of theology in the Erfurt monastery when Luther entered upon his monastic career; it was preached by the Indulgence sellers; it was specially valuable in securing good sales of Indulgences and therefore in increasing the papal profits. It lay at the basis of that whole doctrine and practice of Indulgences which confronted Luther when he felt himself compelled to attack them.

The practice of Indulgences, on whatever theory they were upheld, had enmeshed the whole penitentiary system of the Church in the thirteenth, fourteenth, and fifteenth centuries. The papal power was at first sparingly used. It is true that in 1095 Pope Urban II promised an Indulgence to the Crusaders such as had never before been heard of—namely, a plenary Indulgence or a complete remission of all imposed canonical penances—but it was not until the thirteenth and fourteenth centuries that Indulgences were lavished by the Pope even more unsparingly than they had been previously by the Bishops. From the beginning of the thirteenth century they were promised in order to find recruits for wars against heretics, such as the Albigenses, against opponents of papal political schemes—in short to recruit the papal armies for wars of all kinds. They were granted freely to the religious Orders, either for the benefits of the members or as rewards to the faithful who visited their churches and made contributions to their funds. They were bestowed on special churches or cathedrals, or on altars in churches, and had the effect of endowments. They were given to hospitals, and for the rebuilding, repair, and upkeep of bridges—the Elector had one attached to his bridge at Torgau and had employed Tetzel to preach its benefits. They were attached to special collections of relics to be earned by the faithful who visited the shrines. In short it is difficult to say to what they were not given and for what money-getting purpose they had not been employed. The Fuggers amassed much of their wealth from commissions received in managing these Indulgences. But perhaps it may be said that the Indulgence system reached its height in the great Jubilee Indulgences which were granted by successive Popes beginning with Boniface VIII. They were first bestowed on pilgrims who actually visited Rome and prayed at prescribed times within certain churches; then, the same Indulgence came to be bestowed on persons who were willing to give at least what a journey to Rome would have cost them; and in the end they could be had on much easier terms. Wherever Indulgences are met with they are surrounded with a sordid system of money-getting; and, as Luther said in a sermon which he preached on the subject before he had prepared his Theses, they were a very grievous instrument to be placed in the hands of avarice.

The theories of theologians had always followed the custom of the Church; Indulgences existed and had to be explained. This is the attitude of the two great Schoolmen, Bonaventura and Thomas Aquinas, who did more than any other theologians to provide a theological basis for the practice. The practice itself had altered and new explanations had been made to suit the alterations. It is needless to say that the theological explanations did not always agree, and that sometimes the terms of the proclamation of an Indulgence went beyond the theories of many of the theological defenders of the system. To take one instance. Did an Indulgence give remission for the guilt of sin or only for certain penalties attached to sinful deeds? This is a matter still keenly debated. The theory adopted by all defenders of Indulgences who have written on the subject since the Council of Trent is that guilt (*culpa*) and eternal punishment are dealt with in the Sacrament of Penance; and that Indulgences have to do with temporal punishments only, including under that phrase the penalties of Purgatory. It is also to be admitted that this modern opinion is confirmed by the most eminent medieval theologians before the Council of Trent. Those admissions, however, do not settle the question. Medieval theology did not create Indulgences; it only followed and tried to justify the practices of Popes

CH. IV.

and the Roman Curia—a confessedly difficult task. The question still remains whether the official documents did not assert that Indulgences did remove guilt as well as penalty of the temporal kind. If documents granting Indulgences, published after the Sacrament of Penance had been formulated, be examined, it will be found that many of them, while proclaiming the Indulgence and its benefits, make no mention of the necessity of previous confession and priestly absolution; that others expressly assert that the Indulgence confers a remission of guilt (*culpa*) as well as penalty; and that very many, especially in the Jubilee times, use language which inevitably led intelligent laymen (Dante for example) to believe that the Indulgence remitted the guilt as well as the penalties of actual sins; and when all due allowance has been made it is very difficult to avoid the conclusion that Indulgences had been declared on the highest authority to be efficacious for the removal of the guilt of sins in the presence of God.

Luther however approached the whole question not from the side of theological theory but from its practical moral effect on the minds of the common people, who were not theologians and on whom refined distinctions were thrown away; and the evidence that the people believed that the Indulgence remitted the guilt as well as the penalties of sins is overwhelming. Putting aside the statements or views of Hus, Wiclif, and the *Piers Plowman* series of poems, contemporary chroniclers are found describing Indulgences given for crusades or in times of Jubilee as remissions of guilt as well as of penalty; contemporary preachers dwelt on the distinction between the partial and the plenary Indulgence, asserted that the latter meant remission of guilt as well as of penalty, and explained their statements by insisting that the plenary Indulgence included within it the Sacrament of Penance; the popular guide-books written for pilgrims to Rome and Compostella spread the popular ideas about Indulgences, and this without any interference from the ecclesiastical authorities. The *Mirabilia Romae*, a very celebrated guide-book for pilgrims to Rome, which had gone through nineteen Latin and twelve German editions before the year 1500, says expressly that every pilgrim who visits the Lateran has forgiveness of all sins, of guilt as well as of penalty, and makes the same statement about the virtues of the Indulgences given to other shrines. The popular belief was so well acknowledged that even Councils had to excuse themselves from having fostered it, and did so by laying the blame on the preachers and sellers of Indulgences, or, like the Council of Constance, impeached the Pope and compelled him to confess that he had granted Indulgences for the remission of guilt as well as of penalty. This widespread popular belief justified the attitude taken up by Luther.

But if it be granted that the intelligent belief of the Church as found in the writings of its most respected theologians was that the Indulgence remitted the penalty and not the guilt of sin, it is well to notice what this meant. Since the formulation of the doctrine of the Sacrament of Penance, the theory had been that all guilt of sin and all eternal punishment were remitted in the priestly Absolution which followed the confession of the penitent. The Sacrament of Penance had abolished guilt and hell. But there remained actual sins to be punished because the righteousness of God demanded it, and this was done in the temporal pains of Purgatory. The "common man," if he thought at all on the matter, might be excused if he considered that guilt and hell, if taken away by the one hand, were restored by the other, and that the whole series of questions discussed by the theologians amounted to little more than dialectical fencing with phrases. He was taught and he believed that punishment awaited him for his sins—and a temporal punishment which might last thousands of years was not very different from an eternal one in his eyes. With these thoughts the Indulgence was offered to him as a sure way of easing his conscience and avoiding the punishment which he knew to be deserved. He had only to pay a sum of money and perform the canonical good deed enjoined, whatever it might be, and he had the remission of his punishment and the sense that God's justice was satisfied. It was this practical ethical effect of the Indulgences, and not the theological explanations about them, which stirred Luther to make his protest.

Luther's Theses, in their lack of precise theological definition and of logical arrangement, are singularly unlike what might have been expected from a professional theologian; and they contain repetitions which might easily have been avoided. They are not a clearly reasoned statement of a theological doctrine; still less are they the programme of a scheme of reformation. They are simply ninety-five sledge-hammer blows directed against the most flagrant ecclesiastical abuse of the age. They look like the utterance of a man who was in close contact with the people, who had been shocked at statements made by the preachers of the Indulgence, who had read a good deal of the current theological opinions published in defence of Indulgences, and had noted several views which he longed to contradict as publicly as possible. They are prefaced with the expression of love and desire to elucidate the truth. They read as if they were addressed to the "common man" and appealed to his common sense of spiritual things. Luther had told the assembly of clergy, who met at Leitzkau in 1512 to discuss the affairs of the Church, that every true reformation must begin with individual men, and that it must have for its centre the regenerate heart, for its being an awakening faith, and for its inspiration the preaching of a pure Gospel.

The note which he sounded in this, his earliest utterance which has come down to us, is re-echoed in the Theses. It is heard in the opening sentences. The penitence which Christ requires is something more than a momentary expression of sorrow; it is an habitual thing which lasts continuously during the whole of the believer's life; outward deeds of penitence are necessary to manifest the real penitence which is inward and which is the source of a continuous mortification of the flesh; confession is also a necessary thing because the true penitent must be prepared to humble himself; but the one thing needful is the godly contrition of the heart. In the Theses Luther makes six distinct assertions about Indulgences and their efficacy:—(1) Indulgence is and can only be the remission of a canonical penalty; the Church can remit what the Church has imposed; it cannot remit what God has imposed. (2) An Indulgence can never remit guilt; the Pope himself is unable to do this. (3) It cannot remit the divine punishment for sin—God keeps that in His own hands. (4) It has no application to souls in Purgatory; for penalties imposed by the Church can only refer to the living; death dissolves them; all that the Pope can do for souls in Purgatory is by prayer and not by any power of keys. (5) The Christian who has true repentance has already received pardon from God altogether apart from an Indulgence and does not need it; and Christ demands this true repentance from everyone. (6) The Treasure of Merits has never been properly defined, and is not understood by the people; it cannot be the merits of Christ and the Saints, because these act without any intervention from the Pope; it can mean nothing more than that the Pope, having the power of the keys, can remit Satisfactions imposed by the Church; the true treasure of merits is the holy Gospel of the grace of God.

The Theses had a circulation which for the times was unprecedented. They were known all over Germany, Myconius assures us, within a fortnight. This popularity was no doubt partly due to the growing dislike of papal methods of gaining money; but there must have been more than that in it; Luther was only uttering aloud what thousands of pious Germans had been thinking. The lack of all theological treatment must have increased their popularity. The sentences were plain and easily understood. They kept within the field of simple religious and moral truth. Their effect was so immediate that the sales of Indulgences began to decline. The Theses appealed to all those who had been brought up in the simple evangelical family piety and who had not forsaken it; and they appealed also to all who shared that non-ecclesiastical piety which had been rising and spreading during the last decades of the fifteenth century. Both these forces, purely religious, at once rallied round the author.

Theologians were provokingly silent about the Theses. Luther's intimate friends, who agreed with his opinions, thought that he had acted with great rashness. His Bishop had told him that he saw nothing to object to in his declarations, but advised him to write no more on the subject. Before the end of the year Tetzel published Counter-Theses, written for him by Conrad Wimpina, of Frankfort on the Oder. John Eck (Maier), by far the ablest of Luther's opponents, had in circulation, though probably unpublished, an answer, entitled *Obelisks*, which was in

Luther's hands as early as March 4, 1518, and was probably answered by Luther on March 24, although the answer was not published until August. The Theses had been sent to Rome by the Archbishop of Mainz. The Pope, Leo X, thinking that they represented a merely monkish quarrel, contented himself with asking the General of the Augustinian Eremites to keep things quiet among his monks. But at Rome, Silvester Mazzolini, called Prierias (from his birthplace, Prierio), a Dominican, Papal Censor for the Roman Province and an Inquisitor, was profoundly dissatisfied with Luther's declarations, and answered them in a book entitled *A Dialogue about the power of the Pope, against the Presumptuous Conclusions of Martin Luther*. In April, 1518, the Augustinian Eremites held their usual annual chapter at Heidelberg, and Luther went there in spite of many warnings that his life was not safe out of Wittenberg. At these general chapters some time was always spent in theological discussion, and Luther at last heard his Theses temperately discussed. He found the opposition to his views much stronger than he had expected, but the real discussion so pleased him that he returned to Wittenberg much strengthened and comforted. On his return he began a general answer to his opponents. The book, *Resolutiones*, was probably the most carefully prepared of all Luther's writings. It was meditated over long and rewritten several times. It contains an interesting and partly biographical dedication to Staupitz; it is addressed to the Pope; it sets forth a detailed defence of the author's ninety-five conclusions on the subject of Indulgences.

If we concern ourselves with the central position in the attacks made on Luther's Theses it will be found that they amount to this; that Indulgences are simply a particular case of the use of the ordinary power placed in the hands of the Pope and are whatever the Pope means them to be, and that no discussion about the precise kind of efficacy which may be in their use is to be tolerated. The Roman Church is virtually the Universal Church, and the Pope is practically the Roman Church. Hence as the representative of the Roman Church, which in turn represents the Universal Church, the Pope, when he acts officially, cannot err. Official decisions are given in actions as well as in words, and custom has the force of law. Therefore whoever objects to such long-established customs as Indulgences is a heretic and does not deserve to be heard. Luther, in his Theses and still more in his *Resolutiones*, had repudiated all the additions made to the theory and practice of Indulgences founded on papal action during the three centuries past, and all the scholastic subtleties which had attempted to justify those practices. The answers of his opponents, and especially of Prierias, had barred all such discussion by declaring that ecclesiastical usages were matters of faith, and by interposing the official infallibility of the Bishop of Rome. Had the question been one of intellectual speculation only, it is probable that the Pope would not have placed himself behind his too zealous supporters. The Church was accustomed to the presence of various schools of theology with differing opinions; but the Curia had always been extremely sensitive about Indulgences; they were the source of an enormous revenue, and anything which checked their sale would have caused financial embarrassment. Hence it is scarcely to be wondered at that Pope Leo summoned Luther to Rome to answer for his attack on the system of Indulgences.

This sudden summons (July, 1518) to appear before the Inquisitorial Office could be represented as an affront to Wittenberg; and Luther wrote to Spalatin, the Elector's chaplain, and the chief link between his Court and the University, suggesting that German princes ought to defend the rights of German universities attacked in his person. Spalatin immediately wrote to the Elector Frederick and to the Emperor Maximilian, both of whom were at Augsburg at the time. The Elector was jealous of the rights of his University, and he had a high regard for Luther, who had done so much to make his University the flourishing seat of learning it had become. The Emperor's keen political vision discerned a useful if obscure ally in the young German theologian. "Luther is sure to begin a game with the priests," he said; "the Elector should take good care of that monk, for he will be useful to us some day." So the Pope was urged to suspend the summons and grant Luther a trial on German soil. The matter was left in the hands of the Pope's Legate in Germany, Cajetan (Thomas de Vio), and Luther was ordered to present himself before that official at Augsburg.

When Luther had nailed his Theses to the door of the Castle Church at Wittenberg he had been a solitary monk driven imperiously by his conscience to act alone and afraid to compromise any of his friends. It must have been with very different feelings that he started on his journey to meet the Cardinal-Legate at Augsburg. He knew that the Theses had won for him numberless sympathisers. His correspondence shows that his University was with him to a man. The students were enthusiastic and thronged his class-room. His theology—theology based on the Holy Scriptures and on Augustine and Bernard—was spreading rapidly through the convents of his Order in Germany and even in the Netherlands. Melanchthon had come to Wittenberg on the 25th of August; he had begun to lecture on Homer and on the Epistle to Titus; and Luther was exulting in the thought that his University would soon show German scholarship able to match itself against the Italian. The days were fast disappearing, he wrote, when the Romans could cheat the Germans with their intrigues, trickeries, and treacheries; treat them as blockheads and boors; and gull them continuously and shamelessly. As for the Pope, he was not to be moved by what pleased or displeased his Holiness. The Pope was a man as Luther himself was; and many a Pope had been guilty not merely of errors but of crimes. At quieter moments, however, he was oppressed with the thought that it had been laid on him who hated publicity, who loved to keep quiet and teach his students and preach to his people, to stand forth as he had felt compelled to do. The patriot, the prophet of a new era, the humble, almost shrinking Christian monk—all these characters appear in his correspondence with his intimates in the autumn of 1518.

The Diet, which had just closed when Luther reached Augsburg, had witnessed some brilliant scenes. A Cardinal's hat had been bestowed on the Archbishop of Mainz with all gorgeous solemnities; the aged Emperor Maximilian had been solemnly presented with the pilgrimage symbols of a hat and a dagger, both blessed by the Pope. His Holiness invited Germany to unite in a crusade against the Turks, and the Emperor would have willingly appeared as the champion of Christendom. But the German Princes, spiritual and secular, were in no mood to fulfil any demands made from Rome. The spirit of revolt had not yet taken active shape, but it could be expressed in a somewhat sullen refusal to agree to the Pope's proposals. The Emperor recognised the symptoms, and wrote to Rome advising the Pope to be cautious how he dealt with Luther. His advice was thrown away. When, after wearying delays, the monk had his first interview with the Cardinal-Legate, he was told that no discussion could be permitted, private or public, until Luther had recanted his heresies, had promised not to repeat them, and had given assurance that he would not trouble the peace of the Church in the future. Being pressed to name the heresies, the adroit theologian named two opinions which had wide-reaching consequences—the 58th conclusion of the Theses and the statement in the *Resolutiones* that the sacraments were not efficacious apart from faith in the recipient. There was some discussion notwithstanding the Cardinal's declaration; but in the end Luther was ordered to recant or depart. He departed; and, after an appeal from the Pope ill-informed to the Pope to be well-informed, and also an appeal to a General Council, he returned to Wittenberg. There he wrote out an account of his interview with the Legate—the *Acta Augustana*—which was published and read all over Germany.

The interview between the Cardinal-Legate and Luther at Augsburg almost dates the union between the new religious movement, the growing national restlessness under Roman domination, and the humanist intellectual revolt. A well-known and pious monk, an esteemed teacher in a University which he was making famous throughout Germany, an earnest moralist who had proposed to discuss the efficacy of a system of Indulgences which manifestly had some detrimental sides, had been told, in the most peremptory way, that he must recant, and that without explanation or discussion. German patriots saw in the proceeding another instance of the contemptuous way in which Rome always treated Germany; humanists believed it to be tyrannical stifling of the truth even worse than the dealings with Reuchlin; and both humanist and patriot believed it to be another instance of the Roman greed for German gold. As for Luther himself he daily expected a Bull from Rome excommunicating him as a heretic.

But the political condition of affairs in Germany was too delicate—the country was on the eve of the choice of a King of the Romans, and possibly of an imperial election—and the support of the Elector of Saxony too important, for the Pope to proceed rashly in the condemnation of Luther which had been pronounced by his Legate at Augsburg. It was resolved to send a special delegate to Germany to report upon the condition of affairs there. Care was taken to select a man who would be acceptable to the Elector. Charles von Miltitz belonged to a noble Saxon family; he was one of the Pope's chamberlains, and for some years had been the Elector's agent at Rome. His Holiness did more to gain over Luther's protector. Frederick had long wished for that mark of the Pope's friendship, the Golden Rose, and had privately asked for it through Miltitz himself. The Golden Rose was now sent to him with a gracious letter. Miltitz was also furnished with formal papal letters to the Elector, to his councillors, to the magistrates of Wittenberg, and to several others—letters in which Luther figured as "a child of Satan." The phrase was probably forgotten when Leo wrote to Luther some time later and addressed him as his dear son.

Miltitz had no sooner reached Germany than he saw that the state of affairs there was utterly unknown to the Roman Curia. It was not a man that had to be dealt with, but the slowly increasing movement of a nation. He felt this during the progress of his journey. When he reached Augsburg and Nürnberg, and found himself among his old friends and kinsmen, three out of five were strongly in favour of Luther. So impressed was he with the state of feeling in the country that before he entered Saxony he "put the Golden Rose in a sack with the Indulgences," to use the words of his friend, the jurist Scheurl, laid aside all indications of the papal Commissioner, and travelled like a private nobleman. Tetzel was summoned to meet him, but the unhappy man declared that his life was not safe if he left his convent. Miltitz felt that it would be better to have private interviews before producing his official credentials. He had one with Luther, where he set himself to discover how much Luther would really yield, and found that the Reformer was not the obstinate man he had been led to suppose. Luther was prepared to yield much. He would write a submissive letter to the Pope; he would publish an advice to the people to honour the Roman Church; and he would say that Indulgences were useful in remitting canonical Satisfactions. All of which Luther did. But the Roman Curia did not support Miltitz, and the Commissioner had to reckon with John Eck of Ingolstadt, who wished to silence his old friend by scholastic dialectic and procure his condemnation as a heretic. Nor was Luther quite convinced of Miltitz' honesty. When the Commissioner dismissed him with a kiss, he could not help asking himself, he tells us, whether it was a Judas-kiss. He had been re-examining his convictions about the faith which justifies, and trying to see their consequences; and he had been studying the Papal Decretals, and discovering to his amazement and indignation the frauds that many of them contained and the slender foundation which they really gave for the pretensions of the Papacy. He had been driven to these studies. The papal theologians had confronted him with the absolute authority of the Pope. Luther was forced to investigate the evidence for this authority. His conclusion was that the papal supremacy had been forced on Germany on the strength of a collection of decretals; and that many of these decretals would not bear investigation. It is hard to say, judging from his correspondence, whether this discovery brought joy or sorrow to Luther. He had accepted the Pope's supremacy; it was one of the strongest of his inherited beliefs, and now under the combined influence of historical study, of the opinions of the early Fathers, and of Scripture, it was slowly dissolving. He hardly knew where he stood. He was half-terrified, half-exultant at the results of his studies, and the ebb and flow of his own feelings were answered by the anxieties of his immediate circle of friends. A public disputation might clear the air, and he almost feverishly welcomed Eck's challenge to dispute publicly with him at Leipzig on the primacy and supremacy of the Pope.

Contemporary witnesses describe the common country carts which conveyed the Wittenberg theologians to the capital of Ducal Saxony, the two hundred students with their halberts and helmets who escorted their honoured professors into what was an enemy's country, the crowded inns and lodging-houses where the master of the house kept a man with a halbert standing beside every table to prevent disputes becoming bloody quarrels, the densely packed hall in Duke George's palace, the citizens' guard, the platform with its two chairs for the disputants and seats for academic and secular dignitaries, and the two theologians, both sons of peasants, met to protect the old or to cleave a way for the new. Eck's intention was to force Luther to make such a declaration as would justify him in denouncing his opponent as a partisan of the Bohemian heresy. The audience swayed with a wave of excitement, and Duke George placed his arms akimbo, wagged his long beard, and said aloud, "God help us! the plague!" when Luther was forced, in spite of protestations, to acknowledge that not all the opinions of Wiclif and Hus were wrong.

So far as the fight in dialectic had gone Eck was victorious; he had compelled Luther, as he thought, to declare himself, and there remained only the Bull of Excommunication, and to rid Germany of a pestilent heretic. He was triumphant. Luther was correspondingly downcast and returned to Wittenberg full of melancholy forebodings. But some victories are worse than defeats. Eck had done what the more politic Miltitz had wished to avoid. He had made Luther a central figure round which all the smouldering discontent of Germany with Rome could rally, and had made it possible for the political movement to become impregnated with the passion of religious conviction. The Leipzig Disputation was perhaps the most important episode in the whole course of Luther's career. It made him see clearly for the first time what lay in his opposition to Indulgences; and it made others see it also. It was after Leipzig that the younger German humanists rallied round Luther to a man; the burghers saw that religion and liberty were not opposing but allied forces; that there was room for a common effort to create a Germany for the Germans. The feeling awakened gave new life to Luther; sermons, pamphlets, controversial writings from his tireless pen flooded the land and were read eagerly by all classes of the population.

Three of these writings stand forth pre-eminently: *The Liberty of a Christian Man; To the Christian Nobility of the German Nation concerning the reformation of the Christian Commonwealth;* and *On the Babylonish Captivity of the Church*. They were all written during the year 1520, after three years spent in controversy, and at a time when Luther felt that he had completely broken with Rome. They are known in Germany as the three great Reformation treatises. The tract on Christian liberty was probably the last published (October, 1520), but it contains the principles which underlie the two others. It is a brief statement, free from all theological subtleties, of the priesthood of all believers, which is a consequence of the fact of justification by faith alone. The first part shows that everything which a Christian has can be traced back to his faith; if he has faith, he has all: if he has not faith, he has nothing. The second part shows that everything which a Christian man does must come from his faith; it is necessary to use all the ceremonies of divine service which have been found helpful for spiritual education; perhaps to fast and practise mortifications; but these are not good things in the sense that they make a man good; they are all signs of faith and are to be practised with joy, because they are done to the God to Whom faith unites man.

Luther applied those principles to the reformation of the Christian Church in his book on its "Babylonish Captivity." The elaborate sacramental system of the Roman Church is subjected to a searching criticism, in which Luther shows that the Roman Curia has held the Church of God in bondage to human traditions which run counter to plain messages and promises in the Word of God. He declares himself in favour of the marriage of the clergy, and asserts that divorce is in some cases lawful.

Appeal To the Christian Nobility.

The Appeal *To the Christian Nobility of the German Nation* made the greatest immediate impression. Contemporaries called it a trumpet blast. It was a call to all Germany to unite against Rome. It was written in haste, but must have been long meditated upon. Luther wrote the introduction on the 23rd of June (1520); the printers worked as he wrote; it was finished and published about the middle of August, and by the 18th of the month 4000 copies had gone into all parts of Germany and the printers could not supply the demand. This Appeal was the manifesto of a revolution sent forth by a true leader of men, able to concentrate the attack and direct it to the enemy's one vital spot. It grasped the whole situation; it summed up with vigour and directness all the grievances which had hitherto been stated separately and weakly; it embodied every proposal of reform, however incomplete, and set it in its proper place in one combined scheme. All the parts were welded together by a simple and direct religious faith, and made living by the moral earnestness which pervaded the whole.

Reform had been impossible, the Appeal says, because the walls behind which Rome lay entrenched had been left standing—walls of straw and paper, but in appearance formidable fortifications. If the temporal Powers demanded reforms, they were told that the Spiritual Power was superior and controlling. If the Spiritual Power itself was attacked from the side of Scripture, it was affirmed that no one could say what Scripture really meant but the Pope. If a Council was called for to make the reform, men were informed that it was impossible to summon a Council without the leave of the Pope. Now this pretended Spiritual Power which made reform impossible was a delusion. The only real spiritual power existing belonged to the whole body of believers in virtue of the spiritual priesthood bestowed upon them by Christ Himself. The clergy were distinguished from the laity, not by an indelible character imposed upon them in a divine mystery called ordination, but because they were set in the commonwealth to do a particular work. If they neglected the work they were there to do, the clergy were accountable to the same temporal Powers which ruled the land. The statement that the Pope alone can interpret Scripture is a foolish one; the Holy Scripture is open to all, and can be interpreted by all true believers who have the mind of Christ and come to the Word of God humbly and really seeking enlightenment. When a Council is needed, every individual Christian has a right to do his best to get it summoned, and the temporal Powers are there to represent and enforce his wishes.

The straw walls having been cleared away, the Appeal proceeds with an indictment against Rome. There is in Rome one who calls himself the Vicar of Christ and whose life has small resemblance to that of our Lord and St Peter; for this man wears a triple crown (a single one does not content him), and keeps up such a state that he requires a larger personal revenue than the Emperor. He has surrounding him a number of men called Cardinals, whose only apparent use is to draw to themselves the revenues of the richest convents and benefices and to spend this money in keeping up the state of a wealthy monarch in Rome. In this way, and through other holders of German benefices who live as hangers-on at the papal court, Rome takes from Germany a sum of 300,000 gulden annually,—more than is paid to the Emperor. Rome robs Germany in many other ways, most of them fraudulent—*annates*, absolution money, &c. The chicanery used to get possession of German benefices; the exactions on the bestowal of the *pallium*; the trafficking in exemptions and permissions to evade laws ecclesiastical and moral, are all trenchantly described. The plan of reform sketched includes the complete abolition of the supremacy of the Pope over the State; the creation of a national German Church with an ecclesiastical national Council, to be the final court of appeal for Germany and to represent the German Church as the Diet did the German State; some internal religious reforms, such as the limitation of the number of pilgrimages, which are destroying morality and creating in men a distaste for honest work; reductions in the mendicant Orders, which are mere incentives to a life of beggary; the inspection of all convents and nunneries and permission given to those who are dissatisfied with their monastic lives to return to the world; the limitation of ecclesiastical festivals which are too often nothing but scenes of gluttony, drunkenness, and debauchery; a married priesthood and an end put to the universal and degrading concubinage of the German parish priests. The Appeal closes with some solemn words addressed to the luxury and licensed immorality of the cities.

None of Luther's writings produced such an instantaneous, widespread, and powerful effect as did this Appeal. It went circulating all over Germany, uniting all classes of society in a way hitherto unknown. It was an effectual antidote, so far as the majority of the German people was concerned, to the Bull of Excommunication which had been prepared in Rome by Cajetan, Prierias, and Eck, and had been published there in June, 1520. Eck was entrusted with the publication of the Bull in Germany, where it did not command much respect. It had been drafted by men who had been Luther's opponents, and suggested the gratification of private animosity rather than calm judicial examination and rejection of heretical opinion. The feeling grew stronger when it was discovered that Eck, having received the power to do so, had inserted the names of Adelmann, Pirkheimer, Spengler, and Carlstadt along with that of Luther—all five personal enemies. The German Bishops seemed to be unwilling to allow the publication of the Bull within their districts. Later the publication became dangerous, so threatening was the attitude of the crowds. Luther, on his part, burnt the Bull publicly; and electrified Germany by the deed. Rome had now done its utmost to get rid of Luther by way of ecclesiastical repression. If he was to be overthrown, if the new religious movement and the national uprising which enclosed it, were to be stifled, this could only be done by the aid of the highest secular power. The Roman Curia turned to the Emperor.

Maximilian had died suddenly on the 12th of January, 1519. After some months of intriguing, the papal diplomacy being very tortuous, his grandson, Charles V, the young King of Spain, was unanimously chosen to be his successor (June 28). Troubles in Spain prevented him from leaving that country at once to take possession of his new dignities. He was crowned at Aachen on the 23rd of October, 1520, and opened his first German Diet on January 22, 1521.

The proceedings of this Diet were of great importance apart from its relation to Luther; but to the common people of Germany, to the papal Nuncios, Aleander and Caraccioli, and to the foreign envoys, the issues raised by Luther's revolt against Rome were the matters of absorbing interest. Girolamo Aleander had been specially selected by Pope Leo X to secure Luther's condemnation by the Emperor. He was a cultivated Churchman, who knew Germany well, and had been in intimate relations with many of the German humanists. His despatches and those of the envoys of England, Spain, and Venice witness to the extraordinary excitement among the people of all classes. Aleander had been in Germany ten years earlier, and had found no people so devoted to the Papacy as the Germans. Now all things were changed. The legion of poor nobles, the German lawyers and canonists, the professors and students, the men of learning and the poets, were all on Luther's side. Most of the monks, a large portion of the clergy, many of the Bishops, supported Luther. His friends had the audacity to establish a printing-press in Worms, whence issued quantities of the forbidden writings, which were hawked about in the market-place, on the streets, and even within the Emperor's palace. These books were eagerly bought and read with avidity; large prices were sometimes given for them.

Aleander could not induce the Emperor to consent to Luther's immediate condemnation. Charles must have felt the difficulties of the situation. His position as head of the Holy Roman Empire, the traditional policy of the Habsburg family, his own deeply rooted personal convictions, which found outcome in the brief statement read to the Princes on the day after Luther's appearance, all go to prove that he had not the slightest sympathy with the Reformer and that he had resolved that he should be condemned. But the Diet's consent was necessary before the imperial ban could be issued; and besides Charles had his own bargain to make with the Pope, and this matter of Luther might help him to make a good one. The Diet resolved that Luther should be heard; a safe-conduct was sent along with the summons to attend; Luther travelled to Worms in what seemed like a triumphal procession to the angry partisans of the Pope; and on April 16th he appeared before Charles and the Diet. He entered smiling, says Aleander; he looked slowly round the assembly and his face became grave. On a table near where he was placed there was a pile of books. Twenty-five of Luther's writings had been hastily collected by command of the Emperor and placed there. The procedure was entrusted to John Eck, the Official of Trier (to be distinguished from John Eck of Ingolstadt), a man in whom Aleander had much confidence and who was lodged, he says significantly, in the chamber next his. Luther was asked whether the books before him were of his authorship (the names were read over to him), and whether he would retract what he had written in them. He answered, acknowledging the books, but asked for time to consider how to reply to the second question. He was granted delay till the following day; and retired to his lodging.

The evening and the night were a time of terrible depression, conflict, despair, and prayer. Before the dawn came the victory had been won, and he felt in a great calm. He was sent for in the evening (April 18); the streets were so thronged that his conductors had to take him by obscure passages to the Diet. There was the same table with the same pile of books. This time Luther was ready with his answer, and his voice had recovered its clear musical note. When asked whether, having acknowledged the books to be his, he was prepared to defend them or to withdraw them, he replied at some length. In substance, it was, that his books were not all of the same kind; in some he had written on faith and morals in a way approved by all, and that it was needless to retract what friends and foes alike approved of; others were written against the Papacy, a system which by teaching and example was ruining Christendom, and that he could not retract these writings; as for the rest, he was prepared to admit that he might have been more violent in his charges than became a Christian, but still he was not prepared to retract them either; but he was ready to listen to anyone who could show that he had erred. The speech was repeated in Latin for the benefit of the Emperor. Then Charles told him through Eck that he was not there to question matters which had been long ago decided and settled by General Councils, and that he must answer plainly whether he meant to retract what he had said contradicting the decisions of the Council of Constance. Luther answered that he must be convinced by Holy Scripture, for he knew that both Pope and Councils had erred; his conscience was fast bound to Holy Scripture, and it was neither safe nor honest to act against conscience. This was said in German and in Latin. The Emperor asked him, through Eck, whether he actually believed that a General Council could err. Luther replied that he did, and could prove it. Eck was about to begin a discussion, but Charles interposed. His interest was evidently confined to the one point of a General Council. Luther was dismissed, the crowd followed him, and a number of the followers of the Elector of Saxony accompanied him. Aleander tells us that as he left the audience hall he raised his hand in the fashion of the German soldier who had struck a good stroke. He had struck his stroke, and left the hall.

Next day Charles met the princes, and read them a paper in which he had written his own opinion of what ought to be done. The Germans pleaded for delay and negotiations with Luther. This was agreed to, and meetings were held in hopes of arriving at a conference. A commission of eight, representing the Electors, the nobles, and the cities, was appointed to meet with Luther. They were all sincerely anxious to arrive at a working compromise; but the negotiations were in vain. The Emperor's assertion of the infallibility of a General Council, and Luther's phrase, a conscience fast bound to the Holy Scripture, could not be welded together by any diplomacy however sincere. The Word of God was to Luther a living voice speaking to his own soul, it was not to be stifled by the decisions of any Council; Luther was ready to lay down his life, rather than accept any compromise which endangered the Christian liberty which came to men by justifying faith.

The negotiations having failed, the Ban of the Empire was pronounced against Luther. It was dated on the day on which Charles concluded his secret treaty with Pope Leo X, as if to make clear to the Pope the price which he paid for the condemnation of the Reformer. Luther was ordered to quit Worms on April 26th, and his safe-conduct protected him for twenty days, and no longer. At their expiration he was liable to be seized and destroyed as a pestilent heretic. On his journey homewards he was captured by a band of soldiers and taken to the Castle of the Wartburg by order of the Elector of Saxony. This was his "Patmos," where he was to be kept in safety until the troubles were over. His disappearance did not mean that he was no longer a great leader of men; but it marks the time when the Lutheran revolt merges in national opposition to Rome.

www.ingramcontent.com/pod-product-compliance
Lightning Source LLC
Chambersburg PA
CBHW071958060426
42444CB00043B/2568